Before you read the book

What is the title of the book?

<u>The title of the book is</u> _____

What is the author's name?

_____

Who published the book?

_____

How many chapters are there in the story?

_____

What is Chapter 3 called?

_____

Which chapter begins on page 23?

_____

Which chapter ends on page 34?

_____

Which chapter is about a parcel?

_____

On which pages can you find out about people who work in TV?

_____

Write some sentences. Say what you think the story is about.

_____

_____

_____

_____

Chapter 1

Vocabulary

1. Fill in the missing letters to make words from Chapter 1.

1. h̲ our
2. D __ D
3. fi __ m
4. scr __ __ n
5. c __ __ sin
6. s __ __ prise
7. ex __ iting
8. ap __ __ tment
9. camc __ __ der

2. Write the words in alphabetical order.

1. _____
2. _____
3. _____
4. _____
5. _____
6. _____
7. _____
8. _____
9. _____

3. Write the correct word for each meaning.

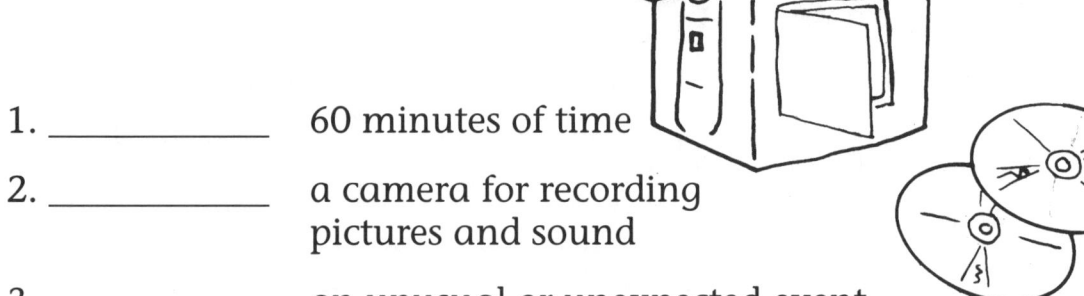

1. _____ 60 minutes of time
2. _____ a camera for recording pictures and sound
3. _____ an unusual or unexpected event
4. _____ a disc for storing pictures and sound
5. _____ interesting and full of action
6. _____ to use a camera to record moving pictures
7. _____ a child of your uncle or aunt
8. _____ a flat for living in
9. _____ the flat surface on a computer or TV

The Camcorder Thief pages 3 to 6

Comprehension

Read Chapter 1 again.

Number each sentence in order.

1   Robert came in the door and put his bag on the table.
___ Steven and Sarah waited on the balcony for an hour.
___ Later, they all watched the film on TV.
___ Robert took a camcorder out of his bag.
___ Steven asked, 'Can you film me playing football?'
___ Robert said, 'I've got a surprise for you.'
___ That afternoon Robert filmed Steven playing football.
___ Sarah asked, 'How does the camcorder work?'

Chapter 2

Vocabulary

> cleaning   covered   expensive   interviewed   laughed
> model   pretended   replied   young   zoom button

1. Write the word that begins with:

1. re _____   2. pre _____   3. inter _____

2. Write the word that contains:

1. pen _____   2. you _____   3. zoo _____

4. clean _____   5. cover _____   6. laugh _____

3. Write the word that is left.   _____

4. Choose and write the correct word in each space.

1. The lady was _____ (laughing, cleaning) her windows.

2. The man _____ (interviewed, covered) the meat with silver foil.

3. A baby is very _____ (model, young).

4. The man on the TV _____ (replied, interviewed) a lady.

5. Everyone _____ (laughed, pretended) at the clown on TV.

6. Steven made a _____ (expensive, model) plane.

7. Sarah _____ (covered, pretended) to be a princess.

8. Sarah asked Dad for a camcorder but he _____ (replied, laughed), 'No.'

9. A car is very _____ (expensive, young).

10. A _____ (zoom button, model) is part of a camcorder.

The Camcorder Thief pages 7 to 10

Comprehension

Read Chapter 2 again.

1. Say if each of these sentences is true (T) or false (F).

1. Sarah and Steven put on a fashion parade with their friends. ____
2. The children asked Dad for a camcorder. ____
3. Dad said, 'Camcorders are too young.' ____
4. The children made a model camcorder. ____
5. The children interviewed a neighbour who had a flat tyre. ____
6. An old man walked up the street towards the children. ____
7. The man was wearing a black jacket with a lion on the back. ____
8. The man wasn't very friendly. ____

2. There are five false sentences above. Write them correctly.

_____
_____
_____
_____
_____

The Camcorder Thief pages 7 to 10

Chapter 3

Vocabulary

1. Fill in the missing letters to make words from Chapter 3.

1. p_ _ nt
2. p _ _ ple
3. r _ _ l
4. ans _ er
5. int _ _ ested
6. str _ _ _ _ t
7. bel _ _ ve
8. sudden _ _
9. fr _ _ _ tened

2. Find and circle the words in the puzzle.

q	t	a	n	s	w	e	r	g	s	k	h	p
z	x	c	b	e	l	i	e	v	e	m	b	w
v	c	f	r	i	g	h	t	e	n	e	d	x
w	q	i	n	t	e	r	e	s	t	e	d	g
t	p	e	o	p	l	e	l	s	p	g	f	d
b	v	c	x	z	p	o	i	n	t	m	n	l
y	t	r	r	e	a	l	n	d	k	j	h	b
g	d	k	s	t	r	a	i	g	h	t	z	f
m	n	b	v	s	u	d	d	e	n	l	y	f

3. Tick ✔ the correct meaning for each word.

1. answer
   a) to reply to a question ☐
   b) to think that someone is telling you the truth ☐

2. interested
   a) to feel or show fear ☐
   b) to want to know about something ☐

3. people
   a) more than one person ☐
   b) animals on a farm ☐

4. straight
   a) real ☐
   b) without a bend or curve ☐

5. suddenly
   a) quickly ☐
   b) slowly ☐

The Camcorder Thief pages 11 to 14

Comprehension

Read Chapter 3 again.

There is something wrong with each of these sentences. Write each sentence correctly.

1. 'I don't like people filming me,' said the lady.
   'I don't like people filming me,' said the man.

2. 'It isn't a real camera,' said Sarah.

3. 'I've got a real camcorder in my car,' the man said.

4. The children were frightened and walked off.

5. The man saw Robert in the apartment.

6. That evening Robert was filming in the street.

7. A car drove slowly up behind Robert.

8. Suddenly, a face looked out of the car window.

9. Steven shouted, 'Look at me!'

10. Robert ran out of the way.

Chapter 4

Vocabulary

1. Match each 'mixed-up' word with the correct word.

   1. hobgut   [d]   a) customer
   2. mustcore [ ]   b) hurt
   3. cribdedes [ ]   c) mall
   4. ruth   [ ]   d) bought
   5. gliny   [ ]   e) strange
   6. lalm   [ ]   f) lying
   7. terrop   [ ]   g) thief
   8. getrans   [ ]   h) described
   9. fieth   [ ]   i) watch
   10. chatw   [ ]   j) report

2. Complete the word or words in each sentence.

   1. The custom __ __ bought a w __ t __ __ in the shop.
   2. I b __ __ __ __ __ t a new bag for school.
   3. The lady des __ __ ibed the th __ __ f to the police.
   4. I fell off my bike and h __ __ t my leg.
   5. I don't like ly __ __ __ or children who are unkind.
   6. There were lots of shops in the m __ __ __ .
   7. There was a rep __ __ t about the robbery on TV.
   8. I heard a stran __ e noise in the middle of the night.

The Camcorder Thief pages 15 to 18

Comprehension

Read Chapter 4 again.

Match the correct ending to each sentence.

1. Steven ran down to see   [d]   a) as she bought a watch.
2. Robert said to Steven,   [ ]   b) in the mall.
3. Dad had a shop   [ ]   c) 'I'm going to lend you my camcorder.'
4. Steven filmed a customer   [ ]   d) if Robert was hurt.
5. The man in the black jacket   [ ]   e) the thief.
6. A thief took the watch   [ ]   f) his film of the robbery.
7. Dad jumped forward   [ ]   g) the police.
8. The woman telephoned   [ ]   h) and held the pickpocket.
9. Steven showed the police   [ ]   i) from the woman's pocket.
10. The police arrested   [ ]   j) bumped into the woman.

Read the sentences you made. They tell the story of Chapter 4.

The Camcorder Thief pages 15 to 18

Chapter 5

Vocabulary

1. Make the following words:

1. an + other = _____
2. any + thing = _____
3. every + one = _____
4. some + one = _____
5. some + thing = _____

2. Fill in the missing letters to make words from Chapter 5.

1. bro __ en
2. n __ ne
3. noti __ ed
4. an __ ther
5. ha __ __ ening

3. Choose the correct word to complete each sentence.

1. There isn't _____ (anything, something) in my bag.
2. Can I have _____ (another, none) sweet, please?
3. _____ (Everyone, Anything) likes the amusement park!
4. _____ (Something, Someone) is shouting loudly.
5. I want _____ (someone, something) to drink.
6. My window is _____ (happening, broken).
7. I _____ (none, noticed) a hole in my sock.
8. I saw a robbery _____ (happening, broken).

Comprehension

Read Chapter 5 again.

Write the correct word in each space.

Steven, Sarah and Robert went to the amusement _____ (park, dark). Sarah interviewed people as they got _____ (on, off) the Big Wheel. Then Robert and _____ (Steven, Sarah) went on the Big Wheel. _____ (Steven, Sarah) filmed them. The man in the black _____ (jacket, coat) was _____ (on, in) charge of the Big Wheel. _____ (None, Some) of them noticed him. Suddenly, the Big Wheel stopped _____ (running, turning). Everyone thought it was _____ (broken, funny). A girl began to _____ (laugh, cry). Suddenly, a _____ (man, hand) covered Steven's _____ (eyes, ears), and someone _____ (took, grabbed) the camcorder from his hands.

The Camcorder Thief pages 19 to 22

Chapter 6
Vocabulary

> disappeared   crowd   worried   minutes   safely
> sure   news   pressed   stole   mobile phone

1. Write the word that contains:

1. rr _____
2. ss _____
3. pp _____
4. ow _____
5. ew _____
6. ly _____
7. ure _____
8. ole _____
9. ph _____
10. in _____

2. Complete each word to match the meaning.

1. __ __ owd — a lot of people
2. __ __ __ appeared — the opposite of appeared
3. __ __ __ __ __ __ phone — a small phone you can carry
4. __ ew __ — something you can see on TV every day
5. __ __ __ utes — there are sixty in an hour
6. __ __ __ ssed — pushed
7. __ __ ole — robbed
8. __ ure — certain
9. __ __ __ __ ied — felt upset
10. __ __ __ __ ly — in a way that will not hurt you

The Camcorder Thief pages 23 to 26

Comprehension

Read Chapter 6 again.

Tick ✔ the correct answer.

1. Who pushed Steven to the ground?
   a) Sarah ☐   b) the thief ☐   c) a woman ☐

2. What did Steven shout?
   a) 'Come back!' ☐   b) 'Help!' ☐   c) 'Stop, thief!' ☐

3. Where did the man in the black jacket go back to?
   a) the Big Wheel ☐   b) home ☐   c) the shop ☐

4. What was Robert more upset about?
   a) Steven ☐   b) his camcorder ☐   c) the Big Wheel ☐

5. Who came to see Steven at the amusement park?
   a) his dad ☐   b) the police ☐   c) his friends ☐

6. When did Steven watch the news?
   a) in the morning ☐   b) in the afternoon ☐   c) in the evening ☐

7. What did Sarah point at?
   a) the TV screen ☐   b) the window ☐   c) the pickpocket ☐

8. Who asked, 'Are you sure?'
   a) Robert ☐   b) Dad ☐   c) Mum ☐

The Camcorder Thief pages 23 to 26

Chapter 7

Vocabulary

Complete the puzzle with words from Chapter 7.

Across
3. part of a bird or plane that helps it to fly
5. going quickly
6. not afraid
9. people who travel, for example on planes
11. a large amount of something in the air, for example smoke

Down
1. to argue or disagree with someone
2. very big or large
4. something that is burning
7. a place where planes arrive and leave
8. an aircraft with wings and an engine
10. grey, black or white cloud that comes from something that is burning

Comprehension

Read Chapter 7 again.

Read each sentence. Who said it?

Robert

Steven

Sarah

1. Let's interview Steven about the robbery. _____

2. How did you feel when the thief covered your eyes? _____

3. He was twice as big as me. _____

4. I'll film you. _____

5. There is a lot of smoke coming from the wing. _____

6. Hey, look at this! _____

7. The fire service is putting out the fire. _____

8. This is so exciting! _____

Chapter 8

Vocabulary

> at once   clapped   excellent   famous   idea
> missed   quiet   tidy   tonight

1. Find and write the words from chapter 8.

clapped / idea quiet famous tonight excellent at once tidy missed

clapped   _____   _____
_____   _____   _____
_____   _____   _____

2. Choose and write the correct missing words.

1. Steven threw the ball but Sarah _____ (clapped, missed) it.

2. It was very _____ (quiet, famous) in the library.

3. I want to be a _____ (famous, tidy) newsreader when I am older.

4. It is a good _____ (tonight, idea) to take an umbrella when it rains.

5. My bedroom is always _____ (tidy, at once).

6. I want pizza for dinner _____ (tonight, excellent).

7. The children _____ (famous, clapped) the winner of the race.

8. 'Stop shouting, _____ (at once, quiet)!' said the teacher.

9. The teacher said my writing was _____ (quiet, excellent).

The Camcorder Thief pages 31 to 34

Comprehension

Read Chapter 8 again.

Write the missing word in each space.

Dad called the TV _____ . He said, 'My children filmed the _____ at the _____ . Do you want to see their _____ ?'

The _____ at the TV studio said, 'Yes. Come at _____ .'

The TV people _____ when they saw the children's film.

A _____ newsreader _____ Steven and Sarah about their _____ emergency film.

That _____ , the family _____ the children's _____ on TV. It was _____ !

The Camcorder Thief pages 31 to 34   17

Chapter 9

Vocabulary

1. Fill in the missing letters to make words from Chapter 9.

1. ch _o_ _o_ se
2. fav __ __ __ ite
3. m __ __ ning
4. p __ __ ents
5. s __ cret
6. sm __ l __
7. t __ __ n
8. __ __ ispering
9. w __ nderfu __

2. Complete each word to match the meaning.

1. w h __ __ __ __ __ __ __   talking very quietly
2. __ o w __   a large place where people live
3. __ o r __ __ __ __   the part of the day up to midday
4. __ a r __ __ __ __   your mother and father
5. __ __ i __ e   you do this when you are happy
6. __ o __ __ __ __ __ l   very, very good
7. __ e __ __ __ __   something that someone knows but will not tell you
8. __ __ o o __ __   to decide what you want
9. __ __ __ o u r __ __ __   the thing you like best

18   The Camcorder Thief pages 35 to 38

Comprehension

Read Chapter 9 again.

These sentences are all false. Write each sentence correctly.

1. The next afternoon, Mum and Dad were whispering.

    <u>The next morning, Mum and Dad were whispering.</u>

2. Steven and Sarah walked into town with their friends.

3. People recognised Steven and Sarah from the newspapers.

4. There were lots of toys in the window of the camera shop.

5. Steven and Sarah had a wonderful time in the sea.

6. The children's favourite camcorder was silver.

7. The children were happy when they came out of the shop.

8. Dad telephoned the camera shop.

The Camcorder Thief pages 35 to 38

Chapter 10

Vocabulary

1. Find and circle eight words from Chapter 10.

q	t	b	r	e	a	k	f	a	s	t	h	p
z	x	p	a	r	c	e	l	w	p	m	b	w
v	c	f	r	z	a	r	r	i	v	e	d	x
w	q	u	i	c	k	l	y	m	t	f	d	g
t	r	z	p	e	i	n	s	i	d	e	f	d
b	v	c	x	z	t	e	e	t	h	m	n	l
y	d	r	o	v	e	k	n	d	k	j	h	b
g	a	d	v	e	n	t	u	r	e	d	z	f

2. Write the words in alphabetical order.

1. _____ 2. _____ 3. _____ 4. _____

5. _____ 6. _____ 7. _____ 8. _____

3. Tick ✔ the correct meaning for each word.

1. breakfast
   a) to reply to a question ☐
   b) to think that someone is telling you the truth ☐

2. parcel
   a) to feel or show fear ☐
   b) to want to know about something ☐

3. quickly
   a) more than one person ☐
   b) animals on a farm ☐

4. arrived
   a) real ☐
   b) without a bend or curve ☐

The Camcorder Thief pages 39 to 41

Comprehension

Read Chapter 10 again.

Number these sentences in the correct order.

___ The children ate their breakfast.

___ Next morning a parcel arrived.

___ Robert's plane took off.

___ They saw a yellow camcorder and a note inside the parcel.

_1_ The family drove to the airport with Robert.

___ The family drove home again.

___ Steven and Sarah cleaned their teeth.

___ The family said goodbye to Robert.

___ The children opened the parcel.

Story summary

Complete the summary of the story.

Chapter 1

Robert came and showed Steven and Sarah his _____ .

Chapter 2

The children made a _____ camcorder.

Chapter 3

The children filmed a man in a _____ jacket. The next day someone in a _____ tried to take the camcorder from _____ .

Chapter 4

Steven and Sarah filmed their _____ at his _____ . A woman bought a _____ . Outside, a _____ took the woman's watch. Dad grabbed him. Steven filmed it all. He gave a _____ of his film to the police.

Chapter 5

Robert and Sarah went on the Big Wheel at the _____ park. The man in the black jacket stopped the Big Wheel and _____ the camcorder from Steven.

The Camcorder Thief pages 3 to 41

Chapter 6

The man ran away. On the _____ that evening Sarah saw the man in the black jacket at the amusement park. Robert _____ the police. They found the camcorder in the man's _____ and _____ him.

Chapter 7

The next day the family took Robert to the _____ . Steven filmed a plane with its _____ on fire. Sarah reported what was happening.

Chapter 8

Dad rang the TV studio and told them about the children's film. At the studio a famous _____ interviewed Steven and Sarah about their film.

Chapter 9

Mum and Dad took the children to a _____ to look at camcorders.

Chapter 10

In the morning a surprise _____ arrived. It was a camcorder for Steven and Sarah from the TV _____ !

Character profiles

Write about the *characters* from the story.
Write two sentences about each character.
Write one thing he or she did.
Write why you liked (or did not like) him or her.

Steven

Sarah

Robert

Mum

Dad

the man in the black jacket

24   The Camcorder Thief pages 3 to 41